a little book of
FEMINIST
ICONS

T0364012

ISBN 978-0-7624-6344-2

Published by Running Press Book Publishers,
An Imprint of Perseus Books, LLC,
A Subsidiary of Hachette Book Group, Inc.

2300 Chestnut Street
Philadelphia, PA 19103-4371

Visit us on the web!
www.runningpress.com

INTRODUCTION

A WOMAN'S PLACE IS NO
longer just in the home. It's
in the Senate, the Supreme
Court, the art room, and the
laboratory. It's wherever she
wants it to be. This book
introduces the stories behind
the accomplished ladies

adorning your flair. You'll see
that they're styled like cross-
stitch patterns—a nod to a tra-
ditionally female pastime that
has been revolutionized by the
rebel feminists and warrior
goddesses of today.

While these rad ladies may
have lived at different times
or in different places, they all
have one thing in common:
They show women that any-

thing's possible. These heroes and pioneers have fought firsthand to make sure that women are treated equally. There are a lot of other heroes who belong on your flair right next to them—those the history books may have forgotten and those who haven't made history just yet.

CLEOPATRA

(69 BC–30 BC)

CLEOPATRA WAS EGYPT'S last active pharaoh. While she is without a doubt one of history's most recognizable women, she is also one of its most mysterious. Her only likenesses can be found on old coins, and the 200-year-old details of her life are shrouded in mystery.

Across the many different versions of Cleopatra, the one thing that remains consistent is just how much power she had as a female ruler. During her rule, Cleopatra formed smart alliances and had affairs with other powerful leaders. She joined forces with Julius Caesar and aligned with the Romans to oust her brother from the Egyptian throne. Following Caesar's death, she fell in love and aligned herself with Marc Antony, just as Roman civil war broke out. The consummate ruler, she fought for her country until its end.

Cleopatra declared herself a goddess to unite her people,

made Egypt richer while guiding it through turmoil, and fought to keep her homeland independent of the expanding Roman Empire. She was also a well-educated strategist who spoke several languages.

VIRGINIA WOOLF

(1882–1941)

"A WOMAN MUST HAVE MONEY
and a room of her own if she
is to write fiction," penned
Virginia Woolf in the 1929
book-length essay *A Room of
One's Own*. Regarded as one of

the twentieth century's most important authors, Virginia was familiar with the limitations that women faced.

While her brothers received a formal education at Cambridge, Virginia learned what she could at home in her family's extensive library. Still, her childhood was not an easy one. The sudden deaths of her mother and half sister in 1895 and 1897 led to the first of several nervous breakdowns. When her father died in 1904, Virginia had another episode that left her institutionalized.

These early hardships still did not hold Virginia back from her passion for learning. Between 1897 and 1901, she took courses in Greek, Latin, German, and history at the Ladies' Department of King's

College. Years later, Virginia became involved in an inner circle of writers, critics, artists, and intellectuals known as the Bloomsbury Group. This was where she met the essayist, and her future husband, Leonard Woolf, with whom she'd open the Hogarth Press.

Virginia Woolf published her first novel *The Voyage Out*, in 1915. Then came many more novels and essays, including the classics *Mrs. Dalloway*, *To the Lighthouse*, and *Orlando*, as well as the pioneering feminist works *A Room of One's Own* and *Three Guineas*.

Despite her success, Virginia sank into a deep depression in 1941. She put on her overcoat, filled her pockets with stones, and drowned herself in the River Ouse.

FRIDA KAHLO

(1907–1954)

FRIDA KAHLO ROCKED A UNI-
brow with pride. She saw no
need to change her mascu-
line features, once writing in
her diary, "of my face, I like
my eyebrows and eyes." The

Mexican painter broke norms in how she chose to live her life and the vibrant art that she created.

Frida was a rebellious spirit long before she picked up a paintbrush. She claimed that she was born in 1910, the same year that the Mexican Revolution broke out. She boxed and wrestled to stay active after contracting polio as a young girl. In a family portrait, she proudly wore a suit as a teen. One of the few female students accepted at the elite National Preparatory School in 1922, she joined a gang of politically minded leftist intellectuals. When she was traveling on a bus with the gang's leader and her lover in 1925, a trolley car struck the bus and a steel handrail impaled Frida through the hip.

Frida Kahlo started to paint during her long and painful recovery, creating the first in a long line of self-portraits. She connected with famous Mexican muralist Diego Rivera to see what he thought of her work. The two became romantically involved in 1928 and married soon after. They had separate but adjoining houses and studios, and both had affairs. Frida's turbulent marriage and ongoing health problems caused her great suffering that she took to the canvas. Unlike any art that came before it, her paintings were gruesomely beautiful and often focused on the experiences that women silently went through: birth, miscarriage, heartbreak, and pain.

RUTH BADER GINSBURG

(1933–)

RUTH BADER GINSBURG IS known as "the Notorious RBG" for good reason. The Supreme Court justice, now in her early eighties, is no stranger to dissent. The small powerhouse has spoken out against inequality and unfairness throughout her career.

Ruth has been defying the norm since she was one of nine women in a class of about 500 at Harvard Law School in 1956. Ruth graduated at the top of her law class, finishing her degree at Columbia after moving to New York for her husband's job. As a woman, it was difficult for Ruth to find employment in a male-run legal world. When she did become a professor at Rutgers in 1963, she was told that she'd make less than a man because she had a husband with a good job.

The first tenured woman at Columbia Law School in 1972, Ruth cofounded the first law journal that focused

on women's issues, cowrote
the first casebook on gender
discrimination, and cofounded
the Women's Rights Project
at the ACLU. She went on to
argue six gender discrimination cases before the Supreme
Court between 1973 and 1976,
winning five.

Ruth Bader Ginsburg was
appointed a justice on the US
Court of Appeals for the DC

Circuit in 1980 and to the Supreme Court in 1993. In her life on the bench, her dissents have helped fuel social progress.

GLORIA STEINEM

(1934–)

GLORIA STEINEM ISN'T
crazy about being called an
"icon." For her, the fight for
women's rights and equality
has always been more about
the mission. It was her trail-

blazing work as a writer and feminist activist in the 1960s and '70s that made the need for change more apparent.

Gloria got her start in journalism as a freelancer in the early 1960s, a time when newswriting remained an old boys' club. In between assignments on food and fashion, she took on pieces that brought women's issues to the forefront. In 1963 she famously went undercover as a Playboy Bunny and exposed how poorly treated these women were on the job.

By 1968, she was a founding editor at *New York* magazine and worked as a political columnist. Her article "After Black Power, Women's Liberation" made national news as a call to arms for women everywhere. Then along came *Ms.* in 1972, the first national magazine that was controlled exclusively by women.

Gloria's activism went hand in hand with her writing. She actively campaigned for the Equal Rights Amendment, designed to guarantee equal rights to women. In 1971, she joined other feminists to form the National Women's Political

Caucus. Gloria Steinem is still fighting the good fight for equality around the globe today.

MICHELLE OBAMA

(1964–)

LONG BEFORE WARM AND insightful Michelle became the first African American first lady in the White House, she was a young girl growing up on the South Side of Chicago. Raised in a working-class family, she went on to study at Princeton and Harvard Law School. As a lawyer at a top law firm in Chicago, she met her husband and future president of the United States, Barack, and was assigned to be his mentor.

Michelle soon knew that her true passion was in public service. She worked as assistant to the mayor and then assistant commissioner of planning and development in her hometown of Chicago. Then it was on to becoming executive director at Public Allies. In 1996, Michelle started the first community service program at the University of Chicago as the associate dean of student services. She continued to give back while working at the University of Chicago Hospitals, becoming their vice president for community and external affairs in 2005.

In her eight years as first lady of the United States, Michelle continued to work toward improving her community by advocating for poverty awareness, healthy living, and improved education for young girls around the globe.

BOSS

BABE

BEYONCÉ

(1981–)

WHEN QUEEN BEY STOOD in the dark, silhouetted by the word "FEMINIST" glowing in giant letters, it was hard to look away. Beyoncé brought feminism to the masses with her performance at the 2014 MTV Video Music Awards.

And once the "F" word was on display in living rooms across America, it got people talking. What did it mean to be a feminist? And just who did that word belong to? Through her anthems of female empowerment and actions as the queen of the pop kingdom, the all-powerful Beyoncé has shown a larger audience of women that they

could be whoever they wanted
to be and still believe in basic
equality.

From her career in the
girl group Destiny's Child
to her breakout as a solo
artist, Beyoncé has worked
to empower independent
women, survivors, single
ladies, and girls destined to
run the world. Her music,
which is often self-reflective,

and personal experiences have
shown women that while the
female experience is complex,
it's also what unites us.

This book has been bound using handcraft methods and Smyth-sewn to ensure durability.

The cover and interior were illustrated by Anna Fleiss and designed by Amanda Richmond.

The text was written by Lauren Mancuso.

The text was edited by Shannon Lee Connors.

The text was set in Jumbuck and Lomba.